DJ AMBITION

SUE LEATHER

LEVEL 2

SCHOLASTIC

Material written by: Sue Leather

Commissioning Editor: Jacquie Bloese

Editor: Fiona Beddall

Cover design: Ian Butterworth, Emily Spencer

Designer: Dawn Wilson

Illustrator: Craig Conlan

Picture research: Emma Bree

Photo credits: Cover: DigitalVision; BrandX/Cadmium. **Pages 4 & 5:** Image100; Stockbyte; BrandX/Cadmium; Hemera. **Pages 38 & 39:** D. Hogan, F. Micelotta/Getty; MTV Europe; Behrendt/EMI. **Pages 40 & 41:** F. Brown, J. Koch/AFP/Getty Images; MTV/PAPicselect. **Page 42 & 43:** S. Finn, G. Robertson/Getty Images; MTV/PApicselect. **Pages 44 & 45:** Ablestock, Thinkstock/Alamy; DigitalVision/Creatas.

The publishers would like to acknowledge the following teachers for reporting on the manuscript:

Carine Chaput, Collège Ozar Hatorah, Toulouse, France

Kleio Drosou, Vytina High School, Arcadia, Greece

Beata Eigner, GRG, Vienna, Austria

Marie-Christine Jacquot, Collège Saint-Maimboeuf, Montbeliard, France

Adele James, Nea Paideia, Hydrari, Greece

Brigitte Neustifter, SHS Weiz, Weiz, Austria

Gertraud Noeth, Christian-von-Bomhard Schule, Uffenheim, Germany

Theodora Papavasiliou, English Language Centre, Trikala, Greece

Monique Peubez, Institution des Chartreux, Lyon, France

Maria Santoliquido, IPSCP 'Marcello Dudovich', Milan, Italy

Mary Glasgow Magazines (Scholastic Inc.)
Commonwealth House
1–19 New Oxford Street
London WC1A 1NU

Printed in Italy.

CONTENTS

DJ AMBITION

ALI ZURI

Ali is 16 years old. She lives in Tottenham in north London. She loves R&B music. The story starts when she DJs at her school's end-of-year party. She wants to work as a DJ in a London club.

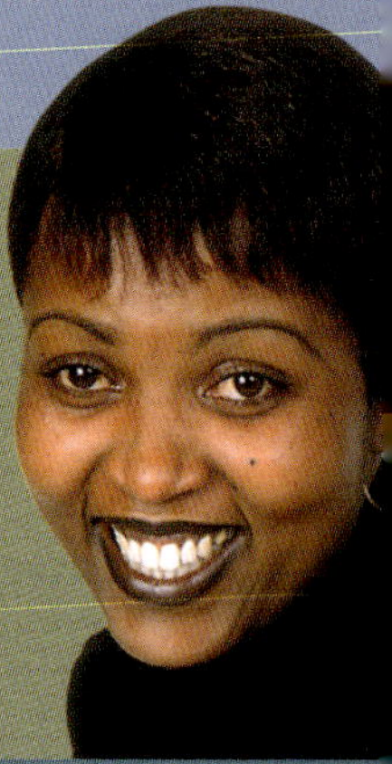

VERONICA ZURI

Veronica is Ali's mum. She wants Ali to go to university and become a doctor or businesswoman.

BEN RICCI

Ben is the owner of The Place, a London club.

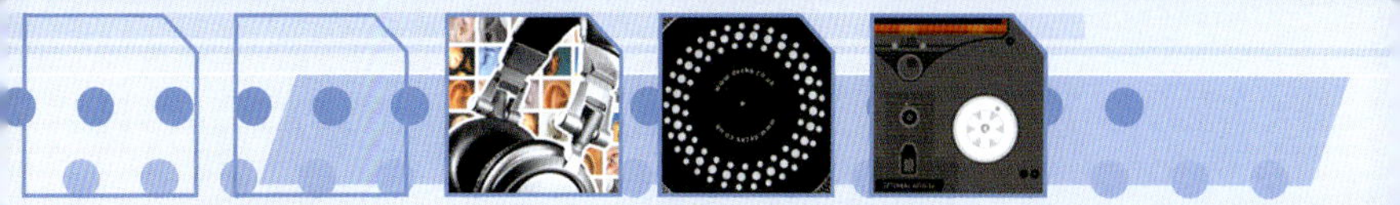

KAT SPENCE

Kat is Ali's best friend. She goes to R&B clubs with Ali. She's also 16.

NIK GALAS

Nik is a boy at Ali's school. He calls himself 'Da G'. He's a DJ and he doesn't want another DJ at the school.

PLACES

Tottenham Place and Westside: Two schools in north London for boys and girls from 11 to 18 years old.

The Place: A club in Camden, north London. People go there in the evenings and dance to R&B and hip-hop music.

CHAPTER 1
A BAD MORNING

'And that was Beyoncé with 'Me, myself and I' on *R&B Today* here at Capital Radio …'

'Come on, Ali. Wake up!' called Ali's mum. 'You're going to be late for school!'

Ali didn't move. She thought about last night at the Foxx Club. Her mum was always angry with her because she went to clubs in the evenings. She wanted Ali to do homework instead.

Ali opened one eye and looked at the clock next to her bed. 7.45. Suddenly she remembered: her first gig as a DJ was only three days away and today she needed to practise! Before she left this morning, she had to collect all her records together.

She jumped out of bed quickly and put on her clothes. She was still wearing her jewellery from last night. 'I'll have to take it all off for school,' she thought. The teachers didn't like earrings or nose rings in class.

Ali got her records then went downstairs to the kitchen. Her 14-year-old brother, Calvin, was sitting at the kitchen table. He was eating his breakfast noisily.

Their mum, Veronica Zuri, was busy in the kitchen. 'Ah, you're here finally!' she said. 'I've got to go to work in ten minutes. What do you want for breakfast?'

'Oh, nothing thanks. I'm not hungry,' said Ali. 'I haven't got much time this morning.'

Ali's brother, Calvin, laughed. 'That's because you've been to a club again, "Miz Ali".' He used Ali's DJ name.

BITION

'You always wake up too late after you've had a night out.'

'Shut up, Calvin!' said Ali. Like a lot of younger brothers, Calvin usually said the wrong thing.

Veronica Zuri looked carefully at Ali. She worried about her daughter.

'You have to eat something in the morning,' she said. 'Here, have this.' She gave Ali some bread.

Ali took the bread and quickly put some butter on it.

'You seem tired this morning, Ali,' said her mum. She gave her a cup of coffee.

Ali looked at her mother. She didn't want a fight today. 'I've got to run,' she said. 'See you later!'

Her mother saw the records next to Ali's school bag. 'Wait a minute!' she said. 'I want to talk to you.'

Ali got her things and walked to the door, with the bread in her hand.

But her mother didn't stop. 'You know, Ali,' she said, 'you're 16 now. You have to make some plans about university.'

'Not again,' thought Ali. This was her mother's favourite conversation. 'Please, Mum,' she said, 'not now …'

'You're clever,' her mother said. 'Maybe you can be a doctor one day, or a …'

'See you later, Mum,' said Ali. She walked out of the door and onto the street.

Her school, Tottenham Place, wasn't far. It was spring and the weather was warm. But Ali felt unhappy. She always felt bad after this kind of conversation at home. Her mother just didn't understand! Ali wanted to become a DJ – nothing else. She loved music. R&B and hip-hop were her life. R. Kelly, Beyoncé, Usher … she loved them all. Ali wanted to do a really good set at the Tottenham Place end-of-year party, her first gig. But she didn't want to stop there. She wanted, more than anything in the world, to be a real DJ in a real London club.

A little way down the road, she saw her best friend, Kat.

'Hey, Ali!' Kat always joined her on her walk to school. 'Last night was great! But I'm so tired!'

'Yeah, me too …'

The two friends talked until they got to the school entrance. There, Ali heard:

'Look at her! It's Miz Ali.'

Ali didn't turn round. She knew that voice. It was Nik Galas. He called himself 'Da G'. He was a DJ, and he was already getting some work in clubs. He thought he was really cool.

'Hey, Zuri!' he called. 'So you want to be a DJ?!' He ran in front of Ali. He was with two other boys.

Da G was tall, much taller than Ali. He stood right in front of her.

'You'll never be a DJ!' he said. He laughed and looked at his friends. They had stupid smiles on their faces.

'Shut up, Galas,' said Ali. She tried to push past him.

Da G laughed. Ali walked faster. Da G was always trying to fight with her. And it was worse this week, because Ali was practising for the end-of-year party. There were two other DJs doing the party. One of the other DJs was Da G.

'Girls aren't DJs, Zuri!' shouted Nik.

Ali walked into the school. She didn't have time for this.

It was only eight-thirty, but it was already a bad morning.

CHAPTER 2
A GIG

'French is so boring,' said Kat to Ali. They were putting their books into their bags. It was the end of their last lesson that day.

'It's *all* boring,' said Ali. She was always waiting for the end of the day. She could play her music then.

'I'm going into town. I need to buy some new clothes for the end-of-year party on Friday. Do you want to come?' Kat asked.

Ali smiled at her friend. 'No thanks,' she said. 'I've got to practise my set for the party.'

Kat walked to the door. 'See you tomorrow, then!' she called to Ali. 'And good luck!'

Ali got her records and carried them across the gardens to the music room. The music room was in a different building from the rest of the school. This was great, because no one could hear the noise. She opened the door. Brilliant! There was no one there, and today the school was open until late. She closed the door behind her.

The equipment at school wasn't very good. The record decks were really old and the speakers were terrible. But it was better than nothing. Really good equipment cost about £2,500 and she didn't have that kind of money.

She turned on the equipment and put on the headphones. Then she started to practise.

Ali played her records. She had a lot of good music: Beyoncé, Kelis, Usher, Alicia Keys and lots more. She practised different mixes for her set on Friday. In the end, she was happy with it. She took off her headphones.

'That was great!'

Ali jumped. She turned round quickly and saw Miss Jakic, the music teacher. Ali didn't like many of the teachers at her school, but Miss Jakic was cool. She was younger than the other teachers, and she was interested in the students.

'Sorry, Ali,' she said. 'I was just putting things into cupboards and I heard the last bit. It was really good.'

'Thanks,' said Ali. 'It's for the end-of-year party.'

'Well, good luck,' said the music teacher. 'I'm sorry, but you can't stay here now. I have to lock the door.'

Ali looked at her watch. Six o'clock! Time passed so quickly when she was DJing. She got her records and ran out of the door. Her mother got home at six, and she was probably waiting for another conversation like the one that morning.

■ ■ ■

Finally the evening of the end-of-year party came. In her bedroom, Ali chose her coolest clothes. Then she put on her new earrings. They were really big rings, just like Beyoncé's. They looked great against her long dark hair. 'Don't forget the 'bling',' she said to herself. 'Bling' was the hip-hop word for jewellery. She was very excited.

She went downstairs. Calvin came out of his room and followed her. 'Well, Miz Ali,' he said, 'the guys will be better than you.'

'What are you talking about?' She turned round and looked at her brother.

'You know,' he said, 'the DJ guys. They're going to be better than you. You're going to look really stupid. Everyone's saying it …'

Ali waited until Calvin got close to her on the stairs. Then she put her face right next to his. 'Shut up, Calvin,' she said. 'You're the only stupid one around here!'

Ali walked to school and thought about her brother's words. Calvin always liked to make her angry. She knew that. But maybe he was right. 'Are the boys going to be better than me tonight? Will everyone think that I'm a really bad DJ?'

When she arrived at school, there were already a lot of people. They were waiting for the start of the party. Kat waved at Ali from the other side of the room, then walked slowly across to her between all the people.

'Hi there!' Kat said to her friend. 'You're late. I was starting to worry.'

'You thought I wasn't coming?! No way!' said Ali. 'This is my first real gig.' Ali felt nervous, but she was ready.

Da G and his friends walked up to them. 'Hello, little girls,' he said. 'Are you ready to see a *real* DJ at work?'

'Shut up, Galas!' said Kat. 'Come on, Ali. Let's get a drink.'

The first DJ, Jaggz, started the party. He played some hip-hop and people started dancing. Everyone was having a good time.

Da G – Nik Galas – came next. He stood behind the decks and waited. Everyone looked at him. Nik did a lot of gigs and he looked very cool. He wanted everyone to remember him. When all the eyes in the room were on him, he started his set. With its mix of hip-hop and R&B, it was really popular. Kat said to Ali, 'He's good … but not as good as you.'

Then it was Ali's turn. Da G walked past Ali on his way to the dance floor. 'Everyone loved me,' he said. 'Now *try* not to kill the party.'

Ali looked away and walked to the record decks.

The students stood around in little groups. Da G was right – they liked him. They weren't happy that it was someone else's turn. And it was Ali's first gig as a DJ. Maybe she was terrible.

Everyone waited. Ali put her records on the decks and started playing. Her first record was 'Dance for me' by Mary J. Blige. Just a few people danced at first. But then, slowly, people got up. Soon everyone was dancing.

Ali played her next records. The party got better and better. Everyone loved Ali's music, and her mixes. When she finally stopped, they shouted 'More! More!'

Ali was hot and tired when she left the record decks. Kat ran up to her. 'Here, have some water. You were fantastic, Miz Ali! Everybody's saying it!'

Ali and Kat had another drink. Finally Ali decided to go home. She passed Da G and his friends near the door. Da G looked at Ali. For once, he wasn't smiling.

CHAPTER 3
TROUBLE

It was Sunday evening when Ali got the phone call.

'Hello, is that Ali?' said the voice on the phone. 'It's Gina Banks here. I was at the party at Tottenham Place.'

Ali didn't know Gina, but she seemed very friendly.

'Your set was great!' said Gina.

'Well, thanks,' said Ali.

'Anyway,' said Gina, 'there's a party at my school, Westside, next Friday. Will you do a set for us there?'

'Well, I … Yes, of course I will!' said Ali.

Ali was smiling when she walked into the living room. Her mother was there. She was watching her favourite programme on TV.

'Well, you look happy!' said her mother. 'What's happened?'

'You don't want to know,' said Ali.

'How do you know? Try me,' said Veronica Zuri. She turned off the TV and looked at Ali.

Ali told her mother about the phone call from Gina Banks and the gig at Westside.

'But Ali, don't forget your school work,' said her mother. 'You can't be a DJ all your life. You've got to think about your future!'

'Mum, I've already thought about it. I want to be a DJ – *that's* my future!' shouted Ali. 'You never listen to me!' Ali walked out of the living room and ran upstairs to her room. These conversations with her mother always ended the same way.

Ali phoned Kat and told her the news. '… and Gina says they've chosen the best DJs from all the schools in north London!' she finished.

'Wow, that's great!' said her friend. 'I don't want to

upset you, but … I heard that Da G is playing a set there too …'

Ali put the phone down. 'I've had enough of Da G,' she thought.

She lay on her bed and closed her eyes. Why were so many people against her? Even Calvin and her mum! *And* she didn't have any good DJ equipment. *And* Kat was going away for a few days with her family; she couldn't be at the Westside gig.

Ali put on her headphones and listened to 'Me, myself and I'.

'I'm going to be my own best friend!' sang Beyoncé.

The words seemed just right. 'Yeah,' thought Ali. 'No one else is going to help me. But I can do it – just me, myself and I.'

Friday night finally came. Ali took the bus to Westside School alone. At the school, Gina met her and showed her the record decks.

'You're playing last,' she said. 'Da G is doing a set, then a guy from Westside, then you. It's nice to have a girl DJ for a change.'

'Thanks,' said Ali.

She looked around. She needed to leave her records somewhere.

'Oh, you can leave your bag over there. Then you can go and dance,' said Gina in a friendly way.

Ali left her records on a table behind the record decks. They were in the right order for her set. Then she went onto the dance floor and waited for Da G.

After a few minutes, Da G arrived with his friends. He was talking very loudly about his set, and soon there was a group of girls around him. They were smiling and laughing. Ali looked the other way. 'How can those girls be so stupid?' she thought.

An hour and a half later, Ali went back behind the record decks and got her record bag. The Westside DJ, Lonnie D, was just finishing his set.

Ali went up to the decks and put on the headphones. She started her set with Beyoncé's 'Me, myself and I'. The song was for all the girls in the room. When Beyoncé sang 'I'm going to be my own best friend,' Ali saw the girls around Da G. They were dancing!

Ali got her next record. She wanted to follow Beyoncé with an Usher song, 'Can you handle it?' She took the record out of its sleeve and put it on the deck. She listened to it in her headphones. But … that wasn't Usher – it was Abba!

Ali quickly took the record off the deck. She got the next one and looked at the sleeve. Alicia Keys. She took out the record. It said 'Army of Lovers'! She quickly looked through the rest of the records. Her own record sleeves had records by Aqua and other uncool bands inside!

Everyone on the dance floor was standing still and looking at Ali. No one made a sound. Then someone shouted, 'Oh, *very* cool, Miz Ali!' Was that Nik Galas's voice again?

She looked out onto the dance floor and felt very bad.

What could she do? Ali played an Aqua song and tried to put her records in the right order. But she couldn't find most of her favourite songs, so she had to play a lot of terrible music. After 45 long minutes, she finished the set.

Then she took her records and walked quickly across the dance floor to the door. Everyone was talking about her terrible set. Ali could see Gina Banks. She was telling her friends something. She didn't look very happy.

Ali ran out of Westside School and into the street. She didn't want to see anybody or talk to anybody. She ran down a side street to the park. She sat down in the park and put her head in her hands. Who did this? Was it Da G and his stupid friends?

'I'll never get another gig,' thought Ali. 'I've got no future as a DJ now.'

CHAPTER 4
THE PLACE

It was three days after the party at Westside School and Ali was still very upset. Kat was back in town and the two girls met at Kat's house. Ali told her friend the story.

'I looked really stupid,' said Ali. 'I'll never be a DJ now.'

'Come on, Ali,' said Kat. She put an arm around her friend. 'Don't worry – of course you will! You're a really good DJ. You know you are.'

'But you weren't there, Kat,' said Ali. 'It was terrible! And how did it happen? It was Da G's idea – I'm sure of it.'

'You're right,' Kat said. 'Da G's friends did it. They were talking about it this morning.'

'Well … no one else knows that,' said Ali. 'To Gina Banks and everyone at Westside, I'm just a bad DJ.'

'*Everyone* will know soon, Ali,' said Kat. 'Because Da G and his friends won't be able to shut up about it.'

Ali looked at Kat. She was right, of course. Da G was probably telling everyone right now about his clever trick.

'Anyway, listen,' said Kat. 'I've got some interesting news. There's going to be a big DJ contest at The Place next month.'

'The Place?' said Ali. 'Is that the new club in Camden?'

'Yes, that's right,' said Kat. 'It's quite small. But everyone says that it's great! Let's go there on Saturday night and have a look.'

'Well, I …'

'Come on, Ali,' said Kat. 'You've got to forget about Westside!'

They could just go to The Place for a look, thought Ali. She didn't need to be in the contest. 'OK,' she said finally.

Kat smiled. 'Great! Now, what are we going to wear?!'

On Saturday night Ali and Kat went to Camden. The Place was a club on a quiet side street. It was already full of people when they got there.

They sat down on the comfortable red chairs between the bar and the dance floor and watched the dancers. 'The DJ's really good!' Ali said to Kat. 'I like his mixes.' Ali looked at the expensive record decks and the DJ behind them. 'Maybe that'll be me one day,' she thought, 'a DJ in a London club!'

They watched the dancers for about 20 minutes. Then Ali went to the bar for some drinks. On her way back, she saw a sign on the wall with information about the DJ contest.

'Do you want to be a DJ? Can you be the best?' said the sign. 'DJ contest: July 24th. Win a residency at a London club.'

'Interested?'

Ali jumped. She turned round and saw a tall, good-looking man, about thirty years old. He was wearing a really cool shirt and green jeans. He was smiling at her.

'Well, yes … I …' she said.

'Are you a DJ?' he asked.

'Yes … er …'

'What kind of music do you like?'

'R&B,' said Ali. 'Some hip-hop too, but R&B is my main thing. I like Beyoncé, Usher, Ashanti …'

'Great!' said the man. 'You've come to the right place. There'll be some R&B later tonight. Have you had a lot of gigs?'

Ali laughed. 'Not really,' she said. 'Just two real ones, and the last one was terrible.'

'Terrible?'

She looked at the man. Who was he and why was he talking to her? He *seemed* friendly.

'It's a long story,' she said.

'Try me,' said the man.

'Well,' she started, 'there's a guy at my school, Da G. He's a DJ too and he doesn't want another DJ in the school. Anyway, he changed my records for some really bad ones …' Before long, this man knew everything.

'… and so everyone thinks that I'm a really bad DJ,' she finished.

'Well,' he said, 'we'll have to do something about all this.'

Ali smiled. 'What can *you* do?' she asked. 'What can anyone do?'

'Well, maybe I *can* do something,' said the man. 'My name's Ben Ricci and this is my club.'

Ali was very surprised. 'Really?'

Ben laughed. 'Really. And your name is ...?'

'Ali,' she said. She was laughing too. 'Ali Zuri.'

'Well, Ali Zuri,' said Ben, 'you need to practise somewhere for the DJ contest next month. What about The Place?'

'I ... what do you mean?'

'Well,' said the club owner, 'we have the very best

equipment here. When the club's closed, none of our DJs use it. So you can come and practise here.'

'Well, I …' Ali knew already that the decks were really good, and really expensive.

'Is that a 'yes'?'

'Well, I need to think,' she said. 'Give me a few minutes.' Ali wanted to talk to Kat about this.

'OK, fine,' he said. 'Come and find me at the bar, sweetheart.'

She looked up at him. 'Sweetheart?' she thought. 'That's a bit strange. I'm not his girlfriend.' Then she hurried back to Kat.

'Where have you been?' asked her friend. 'You disappeared for about 20 minutes. I was starting to worry …' Kat stopped talking and looked at her friend carefully. 'What's happened?' she asked.

Ali told Kat about her conversation with Ben Ricci.

'… but I'm not sure about him. He called me 'sweetheart',' she finished.

'I don't care,' said Kat. 'Ali, this is a real piece of luck. There's no question about it. You have got to say yes!'

Kat was right: Ali was lucky. The Place was a fantastic club. She could practise here on great equipment. Then she could be in the DJ contest. And maybe, just maybe, she could win a residency at a London club! She still felt a bit strange about Ben Ricci. But he wasn't a big problem. She smiled. 'Yes,' she said to Kat. 'Yes, yes, yes!'

CHAPTER 5
A PIECE OF LUCK

'A thirty-year-old man? A Camden club owner?' said Veronica Zuri. 'Ali, I don't like this!'

'Oh Mum, it's OK,' said Ali. 'He's just helping me.'

Ali was on her way to The Place with her records. But her mother was standing in front of the door.

'I don't know,' her mother said. 'This isn't a good idea, Ali.'

'Don't worry, Mum. I'll be fine,' Ali said. 'You don't understand. I *have* to do it! I'll probably never have this kind of luck again.'

Veronica Zuri turned away. She still wasn't happy, but she knew her daughter. When Ali was so sure about something, she didn't listen to anyone – and certainly not to her mother.

Soon Ali was in Camden. She went to The Place.

Ben met Ali at the door and showed her around the club. It looked very different during the day. All the lights were on, and it wasn't full of people.

Ben showed her the equipment. When she tried on the headphones, he put his hands over hers. He didn't need to do that – it was a bit strange. She moved away from him quickly.

Then they looked at the record decks. 'These decks are really expensive,' he said.

'I know,' said Ali. 'They're cool!'

'Look,' he said. 'You turn it all on like this.'

'That's great,' she said. 'It's brilliant that I can practise here. It's a really good club.'

'Thanks,' said Ben. 'I'm happy that you like it.'

'So how did you get your own place? Most club owners are much older than you.'

'I'm thirty-three,' said Ben. 'I got a lot of money from my father when he died four years ago. At first I didn't do anything with the money. I didn't want to make a mistake and spend it on the wrong things. Finally I decided that I wanted my own club. So here I am …'

'Ben, I have a question …' said Ali.

'Yes?' said Ben. 'What is it?' He gave her a big smile.

'Why are you helping me?'

Ben looked at her. 'Why not?' he asked. 'You need help and I can help you. So why not?'

Ali looked into his eyes. Could she believe him?

'Anyway, thanks again,' she said.

'No problem,' answered Ben. 'I've got to do some work in the office now. I'll come back and see you later.'

'OK,' said Ali. 'Bye!' Perhaps Ben was OK, she thought. She put on the headphones and started playing her records. Soon she was lost in the music.

Ali started mixing the records in new ways. Some of her ideas were good; others were terrible. 'This is cool,' she thought. 'The best equipment and time to practise. And I've still got two weeks before the DJ contest.'

An hour later, Ali looked up. Was someone watching her? It was dark in the corner of the room, but she could just see someone near the door. It was a girl. She was slim,

with blonde hair – maybe twenty-five or twenty-six years old. She was looking at Ali and listening to the music.

'Hi!' called Ali across the room. 'I'm Ali.'

'Are you?' said the girl. She didn't seem very friendly.

'Do you like the music?' asked Ali.

'It's OK, but I prefer hip-hop.' She didn't smile.

'Oh, great!' said Ali. 'I like some hip-hop too. Do you work here?'

The girl laughed. It was a strange laugh – almost angry. 'No, I don't!' she said. She turned away and opened the big black door. It closed behind her with a BANG.

'That's strange,' thought Ali. 'Why was she so unfriendly?'

A little later Ben came back. 'Good,' thought Ali. 'I can ask him about the girl.' But Ben started talking before she could ask anything.

'That sounds good, Ali,' he said. He came up to the decks. 'Now, I need to show you something …'

Suddenly Ben moved quite close to her. He touched something on the speakers.

'Er … thanks,' she said, and moved away from him quickly. 'I'm finishing now anyway.'

Ali put her records back in her bag. Ben just stood there and watched.

She walked to the door. 'Well, bye!' she called.

'See you tomorrow, then?' he asked.

'Maybe,' she said. 'I'm not sure about tomorrow …'

■ ■ ■

Ali thought about The Place all evening. Who was that blonde girl? And what about Ben? Was he as nice as he seemed? She was *sure* that he came a little too close to her. But perhaps she was wrong. Was it OK to go there again tomorrow? Oh, she couldn't decide.

She phoned Kat and told her everything.

'But I'm not sure, Kat,' she finished. 'Perhaps he's fine, and I'm just worrying about nothing.'

'Hmm, I don't know,' said Kat. 'Go again tomorrow, maybe, and see …'

In the end, Ali decided to go back to The Place the next day. She wanted to use the wonderful equipment again. And she didn't want her mother to be right about the club and its owner.

So the next afternoon, Ali went back to The Place. When she saw Ben, she told him about the blonde girl.

'So who is she?' she asked.

'I don't know,' said Ben. 'Sometimes people just come in from the street.' He started a conversation about something else.

After a few minutes, Ben went to the office and Ali

started to practise. She tried to forget about the girl. Perhaps there was nothing strange about any of this.

For the next few days, she practised at The Place every afternoon. Then, on Friday, the slim blonde girl came back again. Ali saw her near the door. She took off her headphones and called, 'Hi! How's it going?'

'Why are you practising? You won't win the contest!' answered the girl.

Ali looked at her angry face. 'But …'

'I know some of the judges,' she said. 'You're not going to win. No way!'

'I can see that you don't like me,' said Ali. 'But why? Have I upset you in some way?'

'Stay away from Ben!' said the girl. 'He's *my* boyfriend.'

'But … I'm not interested in Ben!' said Ali. But before she finished the words, the girl was walking angrily out of the door.

CHAPTER 6
BEN AND LISA

'So he's got a girlfriend,' said Kat. 'What's the problem with that?'

It was the next evening. Ali and Kat were in Ali's bedroom. They were listening to music and talking.

'Well, why did Ben lie about her? And why's she so angry with me?' said Ali. 'She really seems to hate me.'

'That's Ben's fault, not yours. You haven't done anything!' said Kat.

'It's not my fault, but it is my problem. She says that she knows the judges in the DJ contest. She's going to talk to them about me. Then they won't make me the winner.'

Ali was very upset. She didn't want any problems with Ben's girlfriend. She thought about it a lot that night, but the next day she went back to The Place. The DJ contest was only a week away, and she really needed to practise.

Ben was in the office when she got there. She started to

practise as usual. She had a new Missy Elliot record and she wanted to mix it with her favourites.

A few minutes later, Ben came in. 'Good,' she thought. 'Now I can ask him about his girlfriend.'

'So, how's it going?' he asked. 'It sounds really good to me. Of course, *I'm* not going to be a judge …'

While he was speaking, Ben came very close to Ali.

She moved away from him quickly. 'Oh, the music's fine,' said Ali. 'I, er … how's your girlfriend?' she asked.

Ben smiled. 'Lisa? What about her?' he asked. Ali looked at his face. He didn't seem upset by her question.

'Well,' said Ali, 'I, er … I met her yesterday …'

'Listen, Ali,' said Ben. He came close to her again and this time he put his arm around her. At that moment, the door opened and Ali turned round. It was Ben's girlfriend, Lisa! She walked out again and shut the door with a BANG.

Ali pulled herself away from Ben and ran out of the room after Lisa.

'Lisa!' she called. 'I need to talk to you!' But Lisa wasn't there.

Ali couldn't find her anywhere. She was so angry with Ben! She wanted to shout at him, but it was only three days before the contest. She couldn't upset him now because she needed The Place for her practice. 'Just three more days,' she told herself. She went back to the record decks.

...

Friday afternoon came. The contest was the next day. Ali went to the club and started to practise. She didn't want to see Ben. She just wanted to think about her music.

Suddenly, the door opened and Lisa walked in.

'Oh good,' thought Ali. 'Now I can talk to her.'

But Lisa started first. 'Stay away from me and from Ben,' she shouted.

Ali looked at Lisa's angry face. 'Listen, Lisa,' said Ali. 'About Ben …'

'I know your game!' Lisa said. 'You like older men. So you spend all your time here …'

'But I'm not *interested* in Ben!' said Ali. 'It's him!'

'You're lying,' said Lisa. 'Ben doesn't do that kind of thing. It's you!'

'Lisa,' said Ali, 'that's really not true …'

But Lisa didn't listen. She turned away from Ali and walked out of the door.

That night in bed, Ali thought about Lisa and Ben. Why did Ben come so close to her all the time? And why did Lisa believe that it was Ali's fault? Did Lisa really plan to speak to the judges? Then Ali couldn't win the contest. She turned this way and that in her bed. She couldn't sleep.

She got up late. When she went downstairs for breakfast, Calvin was sitting in the kitchen. He looked up.

'Good morning,' he said. 'Or is it the afternoon already?! You look terrible. Did you have a bad night?'

'Shut up, Calvin,' she said. She made herself some coffee.

'I've got some news for you,' her brother said. 'You know your DJ contest tonight? Well, Da G is going to be there too.'

Ali didn't say anything, but she felt terrible. She had enough problems already. And now Da G!

Ali drank her coffee quickly. She tried to forget about Da G. She had bigger problems. She needed to get to The Place early and talk to Ben.

CHAPTER 7
DJ AMBITION

At the club, Ali went to Ben's office.

'Ali!' said Ben. 'How's it going?'

Ali was very nervous. 'Ben,' she said, 'I want to talk to you.' Was this a really bad idea?

'Er … of course!' said Ben. He smiled. 'What is it?

'OK, well, I … I want to talk to you about you … and me.' Ali felt stupid.

'Yes?' Ben smiled at her.

'I … I think, no, I'm sure that you, I mean … I don't want you to come so close to me. I don't want your arm around me. I'm not interested, Ben.' Ali's voice got louder. 'And your girlfriend … Lisa … it's not nice for her. She thinks that you and I …'

'What are you talking about, Ali?!' said Ben.

Ali stood up. 'Don't play games with me, Ben,' she said. 'I like you, and you've been kind to me. But please don't do this. It's not right. And it's not fair on Lisa!'

'But I'm only being friendly,' said Ben. He was still smiling, but Ali wasn't.

'You don't really think that, Ben. And anyway, I don't care,' Ali said. 'I want you to stop NOW!'

Ali turned and walked out of the room. 'Now I've got to talk to Lisa,' she thought. Luckily, she found her very quickly just outside Ben's office, at the club entrance. But Lisa was running out of the door. She

didn't turn back when Ali shouted after her.

There were only a few hours before the start of the big contest. She couldn't worry about Ben and Lisa now. She had to think about her music.

First she practised her set one last time. Then she called Kat. Kat was helping her with her clothes and make-up. Kat arrived late in the afternoon with Ali's clothes – a really cool red top and black jeans. The colour of the top looked great with Ali's dark hair and skin.

'Fantastic!' said Kat. 'Now, what about jewellery?'

Ali chose her big earrings. 'For luck!' she said to Kat. 'I wore them at the end-of-year party at Tottenham Place, and *that* gig went well.'

'This one is going to be even better,' said Kat. 'But remember: Da G and his stupid friends are going to be here. Don't leave your records anywhere!'

'No way!' said Ali. She smiled at her friend. 'My record bag's going to be with me all the time.'

'What about the judges?' asked Kat. 'Who are they? Is Ben a judge?'

'There are five judges,' said Ali. 'Ben isn't one, but Lisa knows a few of them …' She stopped smiling.

'Oh, don't worry,' said Kat. 'Everything's going to be fine.'

The contest started at nine o'clock. Between eight and nine, other DJs arrived. Ali was the only girl! Da G was standing around with his friends. They were laughing and talking. 'Probably about me,' thought Ali.

The club was soon full of people. Finally, the judges arrived. Two of them owned other clubs in London. Then there were three famous DJs from the best clubs in London.

'Look!' said Ali to Kat. 'It's Haze!' The two girls looked at the famous DJ. 'I'm so nervous,' Ali said.

'You'll be great,' said Kat.

Suddenly, at the other end of the room, Ali saw Lisa. Was she crying?

'Wait a minute, Kat,' said Ali. 'I've got to go and talk to Lisa.'

'No, Ali,' said Kat. 'The contest is starting in a minute. Don't let Lisa upset you again. Go and wait with the other DJs. Good luck!'

Kat was right. There was no time. Ali went to the back room. 'But what will Lisa say to the judges?' she thought. 'Oh well, with Lisa here I'm not going to win. But I've got to do my best anyway.'

Ali was nervous, but she was ready. Tonight she could show everyone that she really was a good DJ.

There were eight DJs in the first part of the contest, then four in the second part. Finally, in the last part, there were just two.

In the first part she did a really good set and easily reached the second part of the contest, with Da G and two others.

'Great, Ali!' said Kat. 'The judges like you!'

Ali smiled. Perhaps Kat was right. Maybe the judges didn't care about Lisa's stories.

Ali's second set was even better than the first, but the contest was getting more difficult. The judges talked for twenty minutes before they decided on the two DJs for the last part of the contest. It was Da G and Miz Ali!

'I'm going to win, Miz Ali!' Da G said as he walked past her.

'In your dreams, Galas!' said Ali quietly. Da G just looked at her.

It was the last part of the contest – Miz Ali against Da G. Ali felt good. She knew that she could win. She just had to do everything right.

Da G went first and did a really good set. Everyone in the club danced. Then Ali walked up to the record decks and started her set. All her mixes went really well. She started with Ashanti and then played Mary J. Blige, R. Kelly and all her favourites. When she finished, everyone shouted excitedly. The judges started talking.

Kat came up to Ali. 'You were the best!' she said. But Ali didn't say anything. She was too nervous. She needed to know: was she the winner?

Fifteen minutes later the judges had the answer. Haze stood up. The Place became very quiet. 'And the winner tonight,' he shouted, 'is … Miz Ali!'

Everyone in the room started shouting. Ali jumped up and down. She was the winner! Kat put her arms around her and shouted, 'You won! You won!'

'And what has she won?' asked Haze. 'Well, has anyone heard of Igloo?' There was more noise from the dance floor. Igloo was a club in Holloway, in north London. Haze worked there for many years before he became famous. 'Well, give a shout for Miz Ali, Igloo's new resident DJ!' Everyone shouted even louder. 'Miz Ali's residency will be on Monday nights. And she's the first girl DJ at the club!'

Haze came up to Ali. 'Your sets were fantastic,' he said. 'You've got a big future ahead of you.' Ali felt very happy.

At the door she could see Da G and his friends. Da G gave Ali an angry look. But she didn't care now. She was the winner!

Lisa appeared. 'Great, Ali!' she said. 'I'm so happy for you.'

Ali was very surprised. Why was Lisa being so friendly suddenly?

'And I, er … I'm sorry about everything,' said Lisa. 'You didn't do anything wrong with Ben. I know that now. I heard your conversation with him earlier.'

'Oh, er, I …' Ali couldn't think of the right words.

'I was a bit upset after that,' said Lisa. 'I always believed Ben, but … well, that's our problem, not yours. Anyway, you did brilliantly in the contest. Maybe I'll see you at Igloo one day.'

Ali smiled. Finally she and Lisa could be friends. But what about Ben?

A few minutes later, Ben arrived.

'Hi, girls! Ali, you were great! A residency at Igloo – that's really cool.'

Ali and Lisa just looked at him. They said nothing.

'And … I'm sorry, Ali.' He put his arm around Lisa. 'Perhaps you were right this morning, about you and Lisa and everything. I hope we can all be friends.'

'Maybe,' thought Ali. 'But maybe Ben and Lisa will be

happier without me at The Place.'

Then, for a minute, she thought about her mother. 'What's she going to say about my residency?' But all that was in the future. For the moment, Ali was happy, very happy. She was the new DJ at Igloo. This was a fantastic start to her DJ ambition!

THE URBAN

What is urban music?

'Urban music' includes many different kinds of music: hip-hop, garage, house, drum & bass, and R&B.

Eminem : rapper

When did it start?

At the moment urban music is THE most popular kind of music in the world. But it wasn't always like that. Urban music started more than 25 years ago in big American cities like New York and Chicago. It was the music of young black people.

Hip-hop and R&B: what's the difference?

Hip-hop music started in the early 1970s. It took ideas from Jamaican music. Rap is a kind of hip-hop.
R&B music came out of the soul music of the 1960s and 70s. It has a softer sound than hip-hop. But the two sounds have now come together. An example? Beyoncé, an R&B singer, and rapper Jay-Z made *Crazy in Love* in 2003. It was popular all over the world.

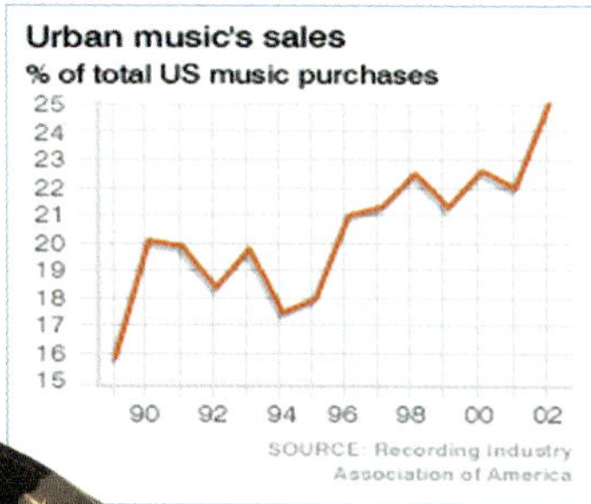

Up and up: the rise of urban music

Missy Elliot : hip-hop singer

SCENE

Who are the biggest names in R&B and hip-hop?

Some of the big names in R&B are Mary J. Blige, Beyoncé, Usher and Missy Elliot. Eminem is perhaps the biggest name in hip-hop.

Where can you listen to urban music?

You can listen to it on the radio. In the UK, the radio station BBC 1Xtra plays R&B, hip-hop, drum & bass, garage and dance hall.

And of course you can listen to it in clubs. In the US and UK, there are good clubs in most of the big cities. Some famous London clubs include Ocean in Hackney, The Scala in King's Cross, WKD in Camden, and The Spot in the West End. All of these clubs have times when new DJs can play a set.

How about the fashions?

Men often wear baggy trousers, hooded tops and back-to-front baseball caps. Some singers, like P Diddy and 50 Cent, wear lots of bling (the hip-hop word for *jewellery*, see 'Can you talk the talk?' on page 41). Sunglasses are also very popular.

Women in R&B music wear lots of bling and make-up. Beyoncé, for example, really likes big hoop earrings.

Mary J. Blige : one of the biggest names in R&B

50 Cent : hip-hop fashions

What's the most popular kind of music in your country? Where do people listen to it? What clothes do people wear?

Find these in the pictures:
baggy trousers hooded top
back-to-front baseball cap
hoop earrings

Destiny's Child: internationally popular

Beyoncé:

Beyoncé is one of the biggest names in R&B. But did you know ...?

1 Beyoncé started the group Destiny's Child when she was only nine years old.

Beyoncé Knowles was born in 1981 in Houston, Texas. In 1990, she started Destiny's Child with her cousin, Kelly Rowland. A third singer, Michelle Williams, joined the group later.

2 Destiny's Child once lost a singing contest.

Yes, it's true. In the group's first year, the girls appeared in the TV show *Star Search*, but lost!

3 Beyoncé's dad was the group's manager.

Matthew Knowles sold office equipment until Beyoncé was 12. Then he left his job and became the businessman behind Destiny's Child.

4 Destiny's Child is one of the most popular girl groups of all time.

They have sold more than 33 million records around the world.

5 She writes a lot of her own songs.

In 2001, Beyoncé became the first black woman – and only the second woman – to win the US 'Songwriter of the Year' award. And in 2004 she won five Grammy awards. No woman has won more than this in the same year.

Find this word in the pictures:
award

What's the most popular girl group in your country? Do you like their music?

the queen of R&B

Beyoncé: blingin'

Beyoncé: 5 Grammies

Can you talk the talk?
Learn these words from the world of urban music!

Yo!:
Hi!

in da house:
in the building (usually the club)

fly:
cool

bootylicious:
really pretty

to shake your booty:
to dance

the hood:
the neighbourhood – the area around your home (usually a poor area)

a honey:
a good-looking girl

a homey:
a friend

bling (or bling-bling):
expensive jewellery; if someone wears a lot of this jewellery they are *blingin'*.

The bad boys of

Are guns and violence part of the urban music world? Some people in the US and UK say that urban music and gangster rap are bad for young people.

"It's a big problem. The words of songs don't kill people, but the violent message is the same from videos and films. It's almost a fashion to kill people now. This is something new."
Kim Howells, UK Culture Minister

Here are some of the 'bad boys' of urban music.

P Diddy

His real name is Sean Combs, but he changed his name to **Puff Daddy**. In 2000, he was in a gun fight in New York. The police arrived and took Puff Daddy and the rapper Shyne to the police station. Shyne is now in prison. Puff Daddy didn't go to prison, but he had to change his name to P Diddy.

P Diddy: 3 names

the urban world

Eminem

Eminem is the world's most famous white rapper. He uses a lot of bad language in his songs. 'I like upsetting people,' he says. President George W. Bush once called him 'very dangerous'.

Eminem: dangerous?

Asher D: prison

Asher D

The garage group **So Solid Crew** are the 'bad boys' of UK urban music. Many of their songs are about violence. Asher D (Ashley Walters) went to prison for 18 months because he had a gun. G-Man (Jason Phillips) got four years in prison for the same thing. And now the police think that Megaman (Dwayne Vincent) has killed someone. Will he go to prison too?

But some people in the world of music speak against gun violence. British DJ and singer **Ms Dynamite** said: 'We must be careful about the words in our songs. Violent songs can be dangerous. My message is this: start loving instead of killing.'

Ms Dynamite: against guns

Can the words of songs really start violence on the streets?

FACT FILE

Do you want to be a DJ?

Follow these instructions and maybe you can.

1 Decide: what kind of DJ do you want to be?

There are two main kinds of DJ: mobile DJs and pub/club DJs.

- Mobile DJs travel to lots of different places. They play the music at parties and for other special nights.
- Pub or club DJs usually have a residency. They play at the same place again and again.

2 Decide: records or CDs?

Some people think that records are best; others prefer CDs. Which will you choose?

CDs are easier to use. They're good when you're learning to DJ.

But many people say that records have a better sound.

3 Buy lots of music

You will need a lot of records or CDs, so start collecting now! But what music will you choose? Maybe you like hip-hop, R&B or garage. But remember – a choice of different kinds of music is sometimes useful. For example, at an office party with people of different ages, some music from the 1970s and 80s will be popular too.

4 Find some equipment

DJ equipment is very expensive – perhaps £2,500 for the best. Can you borrow equipment before you buy your own? Try your friends, or clubs for teenagers.

5 Practise, practise, practise

Practice is very important before you do a gig. Maybe you can practise in a garage, or in your bedroom. Try to meet other DJs in your area and practise together. You'll all get new ideas! Or do a DJ course. Can you find a course in your town or on the Internet?

6 Get a gig

When you've practised a lot, you need to play your music to people. Here are two ideas:

- Does your school have a radio station? That can be a great place to start.
- Make a CD of your mixes and give it to lots of people. Soon everyone will know about your DJ ambition.

CHAPTERS 1–2

Before you read

1 Ali, the girl in this story, has one ambition: she wants to be a DJ. What are your ambitions?

2 What dance music do you like? Do you like R&B and hip-hop?

3 Which of these words are:
a) jewellery **b)** DJ equipment
You can use your dictionary.
headphones **record decks** **nose ring**
speakers **earrings**

4 Complete the sentences with these words. You can use your dictionary.
set **mix** **records** **nervous** **take off** **gig**
a) I've got a ... tomorrow – I'm the DJ at someone's 21st birthday party.
b) There were four DJs, and they each played a ... of 20 minutes.
c) I don't like listening to music on CDs. I prefer ... .
d) She was very ... in her music exam and didn't sing very well.
e) He did a ... of some really cool songs.
f) It's really hot on the dance floor. I'm going to ... my jacket.

5 What is the past simple of these irregular verbs?
a) get **b)** feel **c)** stand **d)** can **e)** cost **f)** choose

After you read

6 Answer the questions.
a) What did Ali do the night before the story starts?
b) Why is Ali upset with her mother the next morning?
c) Why doesn't Ali have her own DJ equipment?
d) Why isn't Da G smiling at the end of the end-of-year party?

7 What do you think?
a) Da G is going to make trouble for Ali at her next gig. What is he going to do?
b) Who's going to help Ali most in her ambition to become a DJ?
i) her mother **ii)** her brother **iii)** she hasn't met this person yet

CHAPTERS 3–5

Before you read

8 Complete the sentences with these past simple forms.

lay **sang** **made**

a) She ... down on the bed and closed her eyes.
b) He ... a record but only a few people bought it.
c) It's a great song, but they ... it really badly.

9 Match the two halves of the sentences. You can use your dictionary.

a) Always keep a record in its
b) I like surprises, so I don't want to know my
c) He DJs at the club every Monday
d) I love you,
e) She'll probably win the dance contest

i) because she knows all the judges.
ii) sweetheart.
iii) because he's got a residency.
iv) sleeve when you're not using it.
v) future.

10 Guess the story. Complete the sentences with the correct people.

Ali's mum **Da G** **Kat** **Ali**

a) ... plays a trick on Ali when she does a set at another school.
b) ... finds out about a DJ contest and tells her friend about it.
c) ... isn't happy when Ali meets a club owner.
d) ... practises her mixes at a club in Camden.

Now read Chapters 3–5. Were your guesses right?

After you read

11 Are these sentences true or false? Correct the false sentences.

a) The Westside gig goes really well for Ali.
b) Ali and Kat go to The Place because they want to meet Ben Ricci.
c) Ben Ricci says that Ali can practise on the DJ equipment at The Place.
d) Ali really likes spending time with Ben.

12 What do you think?

a) Why does Ben say that he doesn't know the unfriendly girl at the club?

b) How does Ali feel at the end of Chapter 5?

c) Will Ali stop practising at The Place?

CHAPTERS 6–7

Before you read

13 What is the past simple of these irregular verbs?

a) win **b)** wear **c)** shut **d)** find

14 What happens at the end of the story? Guess the answers.

a) Who gets a job as a resident DJ, Ali or Da G?

b) Does Ben's girlfriend still hate Ali?

c) Does Ali become Ben's new girlfriend?

d) Are Ali and Da G friends?

Now read Chapters 6–7. Were your guesses right?

After you read

15 Are these sentences true or false? Correct the false sentences.

a) Lisa sees Ali and Ben together.

b) Ali doesn't want to talk to Ben about Lisa.

c) Ali asks Ben not to come so close to her.

d) In the contest there are two girls.

e) The five judges are all famous DJs.

f) In the final part of the contest, Ali is against Da G.

g) Ali is going to be resident DJ at The Place.

h) Lisa knows that Ali isn't interested in Ben because she heard their conversation.

i) Ben finally says sorry to Ali.

16 What do you think?

a) Did Ali do the right thing when she talked to Ben?

b) Will Ali and Lisa be friends in the future?

c) Will Ali's mother let her work at Igloo?

d) Will Ali always want to be a DJ?